Ruggie WealthCare™ Retirement Scorecard

Unlock Your Score to Improve Your Financial Health

Thomas Ruggie, ChFC®, CFP®

Ruggie WealthCare™ Retirement Scorecard

Printed by:
CreateSpace Independent Publishing Platform

Copyright © 2017, Thomas Ruggie, ChFC®, CFP®

Published in the United States of America

Book ID: 170123 00679.2

ISBN-13: 978-1973941699
ISBN-10: 1973941694

For more information on 90-Minute Books including finding out how you
can publish your own book, visit 90minutebooks.com or call (863) 318-0464

Here's What's Inside...

Ruggie WealthCare™ Retirement Scorecard Mindsets

Integrated Financial Planning	Mindset 1
Investment Strategy & Choice	Mindset 2
Income Security	Mindset 3
Consolidated Wealth Reporting	Mindset 4
Life/Long-Term Care Insurance Protection	Mindset 5
Tax Services	Mindset 6
Estate Plan	Mindset 7
Charitable Plan	Mindset 8
Family Continuity	Mindset 9
Simplicity and Peace of Mind	Mindset 10

Ruggie WealthCare™ Retirement Scorecard

The business of Wealth Management has become more and more commoditized over time – that is, many of the services offered by firms managing investment assets have become virtually indistinguishable.

In my own firm, I realized that in order to provide greater value to my clients, much more than a "me too" approach was required. So I took a hard look at what 25 years of experience had taught me about helping clients prepare for retirement. And what I realized is this...

Your health, wealth and happiness in retirement are a function of <u>many</u> things.

That simple realization led to the creation of the Ruggie WealthCare™ Retirement Scorecard.

This WealthCare™ Retirement Scorecard is a tool designed to help you identify and measure (score) where you are and where you ideally want to be, in 10 areas vital to your financial health and comfort in retirement.

Once you understand this, it becomes easier to create an action strategy in which you set goals with measurable outcomes for you and your family.

The Ruggie WealthCare™ Retirement Scorecard reveals how changing your mindset about essential indicators such as your financial, estate and philanthropic planning, investment strategy, collaboration with other professionals, such as tax and legal advisors, can add to your peace of mind in your retirement.

Our clients have found the WealthCare™ Retirement Scorecard stimulating, and appreciate that it requires a level of accountability by all parties. It is truly a differentiator in the value of the experience we deliver to our clients, and I'm excited to share it with you, too.

Enjoy the book!

I hope it inspires you to visit us at **www.RuggieWealth.com** and to take the WealthCare™ Retirement Scorecard quiz for yourself, regardless of whether or not you are currently a client of ours.

I'm confident the scorecard will assist you in improving your financial mindset, providing clarity in your goals, and overall, helping to provide you the financial peace of mind you really want and deserve.

To Your Continued Success!

Thomas Ruggie, ChFC°, CFP°

Why Aren't More People Confident About Their Financial Future?

We all know there are many reasons people put off discussing and planning for their financial futures.

- For many, the very act can seem scary and complex.
- Some may feel unmotivated because they don't really understand how money works.
- Others may fret about the uncertainty surrounding retirement support systems and pension plans. As little as 30 or 40 years ago, most people had pension plans, with a defined benefit or amount of money they would receive upon retirement. They could also count on social security benefits. Now, more and more people have to accumulate their own assets to retire, even with social security. And since they are living longer on average, those assets may need to last 20-30 years.
- Despite good intentions, very few people experience any social or peer pressure to get their financial houses in order.

Interestingly, it may be difficult for your financial advisor to accurately assess how well you are doing, as well.

As a result, many people get piecemeal financial planning. Generally, there's not much coordination between different trusted professionals, which can lead to differing or even conflicting advice.

So people turn to advice from their neighbors, their friends, their golf buddies, and people they hear on the TV and radio. Everyone's willing to offer advice, but not everyone has the expertise, the experience or the willingness to truly understand the unique underlying issues individuals may be facing.

While there's a tremendous amount of educational material out there, more resources do not always translate to more confidence.

When planning for retirement, focusing on one or two indicators to assess how good your financial health is, makes no more sense than focusing only on your blood pressure and heart rate to assess how good your actual health is.

I'm a big believer that if you simplify the process and make it easy for people to gauge how well they are doing in preparing for retirement, more people will get started doing it.

We believe The Ruggie WealthCare™ Retirement ScoreCard methodology provides the right tool for evaluating where are you now and realistically where you would like to be, across 10 different mindsets.

Taken together, these mindsets provide a starting point to understand and improve your financial health in retirement.

How the Ruggie WealthCare™ Retirement Scorecard Can Help You Better Prepare for an Uncertain Future

The WealthCare™ Retirement Scorecard is a tool that was created based on 25 years of helping our own clients prepare for retirement.

Each of the 10 mindsets is separated across four developmental stages and a 10-point scoring system. Everyone should consider each question. However, not every question will apply to everyone.

For example, when it comes to the mindset about tax services, a perfect 10 on our scorecard basically says you have a fantastic tax advisor, and everything is being taken care of. But certainly, some people either have a simple enough situation not to need a tax advisor or have the education and training necessary to take care of their taxes themselves.

For others, the mindset about charitable giving may be less relevant. While a lot of our clients are very charitably inclined, not everyone feels this way. If you're not charitably inclined, the score of 10, which says you have everything taken care of from a charitable planning standpoint may not apply.

With 10 questions and a 10-point scoring system, there's an opportunity to generate a perfect score of 100.

I structured it this way on purpose to anchor your score back to a familiar scale and the way we all thought about how things were scored back in high school or college. The perfect result was 100 and anything below might put you in a B or C category. It's an easy way to translate the score on the scorecard to something familiar.

As with many things, we are looking for incremental improvements and the score you start with is just a marker. A line in the sand.

As you go through the scorecard I recommend answering truthfully about where you are today and thinking carefully about what an ideal score would look like for you one to two years ahead.

Really, it's the difference between those two scores that will identify the pain points or areas that you ultimately should focus on to get the peace of mind you're looking for.

I believe that for some mindsets you'll be surprised how quickly you can see improvements.

Let's use the estate planning mindset as an example. Although you may have all your documents perfectly drafted with everything in place exactly as they should be, you may not have the confidence, at the moment, that things are where they need to be.

All you may need to do is to go through and evaluate the documents you have to give you the comfort and confidence you need that your legal documents are as they should be. If this is an area that has been troubling you, this simple assessment may give you greater peace of mind.

Of course, if there are adjustments that need to be made, they can be taken care of pretty quickly.

In my experience, most people end up with mindsets somewhere between a five or a six the first time they complete their scorecard and I'd anticipate the same for you.

Identifying the mindsets where the gap between your current and ideal scores is the largest is one way to help you narrow your focus to those areas where you can see the biggest benefits.

As you do, taking time to notice how you feel about each mindset can also be an indication of those areas where more confidence will give you greater peace of mind.

What I've found in working closely with the people who have completed their scorecards so far, is that if the scorecards resonate with them they REALLY resonate with them, and they will likely want to evaluate and improve their scores. I've also found that when they don't resonate with someone, it can be a sign that our financial philosophies differ, and though they will derive benefit from the exercise, they're probably not a good fit for the way we work and how we can best serve them. It helps us, as well as our potential clients, determine if we're a good fit for each other.

Completing this scorecard will give you an indication of the areas of your financial life where more attention will provide more confidence.

And, with the scorecard to guide us, we can help you track your progress over time. It helps us to be more accountable too.

I truly believe this scorecard will have a huge impact on you even if we never meet or have the chance to work together.

Now let's get started.

Mindset Number One:
Integrated Financial Planning

Mindset 1: Integrated Financial Planning	
You do not have a trusted advisor, nor coordination of your financial strategies, or you "do it yourself"	1 2 3
You have one or more advisors but not one you are confident has provided you with the necessary integrated financial strategies	4 5 6
You have a trusted advisor, but you are uncertain your advisor has the capacity to thoroughly take care of all your integrated financial planning needs	7 8 9
You have a trusted advisor you are confident has implemented the best strategy and has the team in place to meet all your integrated financial planning needs	10

Score:	
Ideal:	

Mindset number one addresses integrated financial planning. The first column simply says **you do not have a trusted advisor or coordination of your financial strategies, or you do it yourself**. For many people this is the starting place. Having a trusted advisor or coordination of your financial strategies may not be something you have considered yet. Or you may be happy searching for information yourself.

Column two states **you have one or more financial advisors, but not one you are confident has provided you with the necessary integrated financial strategies.** As you progress, you often find that comprehensive answers are hard to find online. You may have started to seek advice, but have not found a financial advisor you consider to be a part of your team yet.

Column three, **you have a trusted advisor, but you are uncertain your advisor has the capacity to thoroughly take care of all your integrated financial planning needs.** This is where most people who believe they have their financial planning needs covered find themselves. You are working with one or more trusted advisors who are not necessarily connected. You lack someone who takes a holistic view of all your needs, or you are trying to fill that role yourself.

Column four, **you have a trusted advisor you are confident has implemented the best strategy and has the best team in place to meet all of your integrated financial needs.** This is the stage at which you achieve financial confidence. Your team is in place and you are confident they are taking care of the complete picture.

The key here, as you can pick up from each of the four columns, is to have a trusted advisor who can assist in all areas of your overall wealth management plan as you head toward retirement and beyond. This is the real reason the scorecard was developed, and it is a true value-add for people who adopt the process. Think of a trusted advisor as your personal chief financial officer (CFO).

It takes a team to make all of this come together. Just like any sports team out there, you need good owners, good coaches, good team leaders and team members all working together for the good of the team.

This approach ensures the team is heading in a winning direction and has an integrated approach to success.

Mindset Number Two: Investment Strategy & Choice

Mindset 2: Investment Strategy & Choice	
Your financial advisor(s) has limited capacity to evaluate all available options (for example, insurance license only)	1 2 3
You do not know if your financial advisor has the ability to provide investment recommendations autonomously	4 5 6
Your trusted advisor has the ability to recommend virtually any investments but you are still concerned about bias	7 8 9
Your trusted advisor has the resources to recommend and evaluate all traditional investments as well as alternative investments	10

Score:	
Ideal:	

The first column says **your financial advisor or advisors have limited capacity to evaluate all options**. For example, your advisor might be insurance licensed only, and limited in the breadth of experience, expertise and knowledge they can share. This is often the case when someone chooses an advisor without assessing that advisor's qualifications. Unfortunately, something is not always better than nothing.

Column two says **you do not know if your financial advisor has the ability to provide investment recommendations autonomously**. In this case you may have checked the breadth of advice your advisor can give, but you're not aware whether they are unbiased or beholden to a certain provider, company or product line. The ability to look across the whole of the market is usually far more beneficial for offering a wider set of solutions.

Column three, **your trusted advisor has the ability to recommend virtually any investments, but you are still concerned about potential bias**. This stage is approaching the threshold of confidence in this mindset. You are experienced enough to recognize the benefits of good advice but don't have total confidence in the advisor you've chosen. This may be a problem with the advisor or it may just be a communication issue that is easy to resolve.

Column four, **your trusted advisor has the resources to recommend and evaluate all**

traditional investments as well as alternative investments. In this stage you are confident your advisor has a fiduciary focus and is looking out for your best interests rather than his or her own.

The main goal here is to have a trusted advisor who offers both strategy and choice.

By 'strategy', we mean there is a well thought-out investment plan. It is amazing the number of times we've seen clients who've just been sold a product by a 'product pusher' who pedals investments du jour. Often the advisor does not maintain contact following the sale because he or she made an upfront commission and moved on. For that type of advisor, there's no incentive to maintain a relationship on an ongoing basis.

By 'choice', we mean investment choice. We recommend choosing an investment professional who is independent and fee-based.

Having a trusted advisor who has the ability to recommend the right investment helps to eliminate many of the problems involved with product pushers, a problem we frequently see with annuity-based sales people.

Mindset Number Three: Income Security

Mindset 3: Income Security	
You have significant concerns in your ability to maintain your lifestyle and have not developed a strategy to provide you peace of mind	1 2 3
You have a strategy in place but you are unsure if distributions are sustainable	4 5 6
You are confident in your ability to maintain your lifestyle, but do not feel you have a well-thought-out strategy to assure this	7 8 9
You're confident in your ability to maintain your lifestyle and have an integrated, systematized strategy to provide you financial peace of mind	10

Score:	
Ideal:	

In column one, **you have significant concerns about your ability to maintain your lifestyle and have not developed a strategy to provide you with peace of mind.** Someone at this stage may not have made any plans for income security. Importantly, this is especially a concern for those experiencing a significant life event. Illness, divorce or employment changes can all significantly impact what were once solid plans.

Column two, **you have a strategy in place, but you are unsure if distributions are sustainable to provide the long-term security that you're looking for.** Here you have a plan, but perhaps through lack of knowledge or incomplete advice, you are not confident about the effectiveness of that plan.

Column three, **you are confident in your ability to maintain your lifestyle but do not feel you have a well thought out strategy to assure this.** Again, this level is at the threshold of peace of mind. You have a strong plan but there may be one element you're not certain of, or you may be aware there are opportunities to improve the plan you are missing out on.

Then, finally, column four, **you're confident in your ability to maintain your lifestyle and have an integrated systematized strategy to provide you financial peace of mind.** At this stage, you are confident of the advice you're getting. Confident your plan is up-to-date and flexible enough to adapt to any change in your situation.

When I think about income security, I consider that if you are retired or soon to be retired, the best peace of mind you can have is confidence that your plan and investments are going to allow you to continue to maintain the lifestyle you're currently accustomed to without having the concern that you'll run out of resources.

Our team has a couple of strategies we incorporate to help simplify this process and provide our clients with this much-needed confidence.

Mindset Number Four: Consolidated Wealth Reporting

Mindset 4: Consolidated Wealth Reporting	
You do not have a systematized, on-line reporting system consolidating all of your assets	1
	2
	3
You have reporting available through your current custodian but it does not tie all assets together	4
	5
	6
You have reporting through your current custodian and receive a report consolidating all assets upon request	7
	8
	9
You have a systematized reporting process for not only your investments but your entire net worth readily available	10

Score:	
Ideal:	

Column one states, **you do not have a systematized online reporting system consolidating all of your assets**. This is the stage most people without a 'joined-up' plan find themselves in. One account, many tools, many logins, some relying just on paper statements.

Column two, **you have reporting available through your current custodian, but it does not tie all assets together**. You may have access to everything, but it's very difficult to see the complete picture. You have to rely on additional spreadsheets or reports from your banker or accountant to see your current position.

Column three, **you have to report through your current custodian and receive a report consolidating all assets upon request**. Here you have done the work to set up the report types useful to you, but it relies on manual intervention. While this gives you visibility, the process is slow and doesn't give you complete peace of mind.

Column four, **you have a systematized reporting process for not only your investments but your entire net worth readily available**. Having your information available at your fingertips anytime, gives you the confidence to get on with the rest of your plan. At this stage reporting almost becomes something you can forget about as the information is always there, when you need it.

For years, our clients have been looking for a system that provides reporting not only on investment assets but on their entire net worth.

Putting into place a robust reporting system, including a document warehouse where we can digitally store legal documents, tax returns, insurance policies, and other pertinent information for our clients, has proven to be a game changer.

It comes down to simplicity and peace of mind. Our clients know there's a go-to place they can go online, type in their password, and see a listing of all of their assets, whether those assets are held with their advisor, in their 401k plan, even cash assets in the bank. Beyond that, they can see digital copies of all their legal documents, tax returns, insurance policies, deeds, etc., in the same place. Basically, they have convenient access to everything they could need or want to see from a financial reporting/documentation perspective at their fingertips

Another unique aspect of the system is that other trusted professionals can access specific areas, with permission. For example, if clients wanted to have their CPA have access to their tax returns, we can establish it so he or she can have access to that information but no other information that's held within the program.

We found that in fairly simple situations, people still don't have a good grasp on where everything is. Of course, the more complex the situation gets; for example, you've got multiple trusts set up, you have a number of children, you had a divorce, you own or have owned a business, it gets very complicated to try to continuously monitor and track where all your assets are. I've literally had people come to me with a huge box of papers. It is just a mess. They were hoping everything they would ever need was somewhere in that box. And sadly, they were probably the only ones who could even go through it and figure out what exactly they had in there.

Ultimately, you want to know that if anything happens to you or your spouse, especially if you're a retiree, having consolidated access can simplify the situation. You click a button and your financial information is right there, and your important documents are warehoused right alongside it.

It's a game changer and it's very exciting to me to see how much we've been able to provide peace of mind using this system.

Mindset Number Five: Life/Long-Term Care Insurance Protection

Mindset 5: Life/Long-Term Care Insurance Protection	
You have some insurances which have not been properly evaluated or you have not evaluated the potential use of insurances in your plan	1
	2
	3
You evaluated your insurance coverages five or more years ago; things were fine then, but you have not re-evaluated since	4
	5
	6
You have evaluated current and future insurance uses but you are not certain this can't be improved	7
	8
	9
You have thoroughly evaluated all existing insurances within the past two years and have made educated decisions regarding their inclusion or exclusion in your strategy	10

Score:	
Ideal:	

In column one, **you have some insurances which have not been properly evaluated, or you have not evaluated the potential use of insurances in your plan.** Insurance is too often not thought about until it's needed. In the worst case you may not be covered at all. In the best case at this stage, you may be significantly under or over insured.

Column two, **you evaluated your insurance coverages five or more years ago. Things were fine then, but you have not re-evaluated since**. This is perhaps the most common case for anyone completing this scorecard who is not yet working with an advisor who assesses his or her client's situation holistically. In most cases, clients know they need various insurances and have taken some steps to putting those insurances in place, but often overlook the need to periodically reassess their situation and the coverages provided.

Column three, **you have evaluated current and future insurance uses but are not certain this cannot be improved**. Just below complete peace of mind is the stage where you're sure your current needs are met, but you don't have the confidence someone is assessing the marketplace to look for improvements.

The fourth column, **you have thoroughly evaluated all existing insurances within the last two years and have made educated decisions regarding their inclusion or**

exclusion in your strategy. This stage is where your team comes into its own again. A trusted advisor is right there to assess the ever-changing marketplace and regularly present you with options based on your unique situation.

The purpose here is not that everybody needs to have life insurance or long-term care coverage. The purpose is actually twofold. Number one, we want to make sure that if you currently have policies, they are being evaluated on an annual or, at the very least, bi-annual basis. Insurance can be very complex and the nuances can be hard to understand. Many clients have been surprised to find out exactly what their policies cover (or don't), how and under what circumstances they can be initiated, how and when claims are paid and to whom, etc. A thorough evaluation can assess these factors, and knowing what your coverage is BEFORE you need it is critical. So many things can go wrong with insurance policies, and you want to fix any problems before they occur.

Existing insurances are typically not reviewed or not reviewed well. When was the last time you thought about the condition of your insurance carrier/provider? When did you last determine the viability of the term of your contract? Is it going to stay in force as long as it was projected to? And of course, when was the last time you reviewed your beneficiaries? (I can't tell you how many times we've had ex-wives or children who have caused some concerns within the family still listed as beneficiaries when that is not the policyholders' wishes). Frequently, changes need to be made to beneficiaries. Unfortunately, like so many things, being proactive often falls prey to that old bugaboo – 'out of sight, out of mind.'

The second purpose of this exercise is that if there is currently no insurance in place, we want to make sure we identify and examine whether having coverage is advantageous.

We want to make sure we've evaluated your actual situation, and then, from a planning standpoint, determined whether additional plans should be implemented. We will want to examine what the timing for this should be and how any new plans will be monitored going forward.

Mindset Number Six:
Tax Services

Mindset 6: Tax Services	
Your accounting needs are simple and do not require the use of a qualified tax firm	1
	2
	3
You utilize a tax firm but know you need to make an adjustment	4
	5
	6
You have a tax firm you are comfortable with but are not certain they are the best firm for you and/or they do not coordinate with your trusted advisor	7
	8
	9
You have a qualified tax firm to handle your unique set of circumstances, and to coordinate with your trusted advisor	10

Score:	
Ideal:	

Moving on to mindset number six, tax services. Column one says, **your accounting needs are simple and do not require the use of a qualified tax firm**. This stage may well be less about being unprepared, and more about how straightforward your needs are. If your score is low on this mindset because your tax requirements are simple, that is not necessarily an issue. However, if your score is low and you have a complicated tax situation, that requires attention.

Column two, **you utilize a tax firm but know you need to make an adjustment**. There are many reasons you could find yourself in this stage. Procrastination, family connections and uncertainty can all lead to not making the decision you need to make. Identifying this as a pain point may be the encouragement you need to address the situation.

Column three, **you have a tax firm you are comfortable with but are not certain they are the best firm for you and/or they do not coordinate with your trusted advisor.** At this stage you are probably not harming your situation, but there are almost certainly improvements and recommendations you are missing out on. The biggest benefit to someone in this stage is all your advisors collectively brainstorming on your situation to derive the right outcome for you and your family.

In column four, **you have a qualified tax firm to handle your unique set of circumstances and coordinate with your trusted advisor**. The team is working well together at this stage and their unique knowledge of your situation and the skills of the rest of the team mean you receive the best, most appropriate tax advice.

As I previously mentioned, not everyone who completes the WealthCare™ Scorecard is going to need or desire tax services. The key here is if a tax professional is currently involved, we want to make sure he or she is qualified to handle your unique interests and those of the end user if different. Additionally, this advisor should be willing to work with your team to help coordinate all necessary details for your family's benefit. This is a big area where we've really made some improvements for our clients, and those we've spoken with agree this should really be approached from a team standpoint.

We've actually held brainstorming sessions with a family's CPA, attorney, and other trusted advisors all in the room at the same time. We feel that by having this interaction, the outcomes of our discussions focus solely on doing what is in the best interest of the client.

Mindset Number Seven: Estate Plan

Mindset 7: Estate Plan	
You do not have any legal documents drafted or they are outdated	1
	2
	3
You have some basic legal documents/wills but have not gone through a thorough estate-planning process	4
	5
	6
You went through a thorough process years ago but don't remember all aspects and would benefit from an update	7
	8
	9
You have a well-thought-out and executed estate plan that is completely understood by you, your family and your financial team	10

Score:	
Ideal:	

Mindset number seven is the legal side of estate planning. Column one is **you do not have any legal documents drafted, or they are outdated**. Failing to plan, is planning to fail as they say and, unfortunately, estate planning all too often falls into this category. Whether you think you don't have an estate to plan for, or you think it is too expensive to address this formally, estate planning can make a difference in the hundreds of thousands of dollars, or more, to your estate. At this stage, people often haven't realized that.

Column two, **you have some basic legal documents, such as wills, but have not gone through a thorough estate planning process**. Ensuring you have a correctly drafted will is a great first step in the process. People at this stage have realized the importance of this but have not looked at their estate as a whole. Those who don't have an estate plan will usually find there are benefits from even the most rudimentary estate planning.

Column three, **you went through a thorough process years ago but don't remember all aspects and would benefit from an update**. Regulations are subject to constant change and amendment. If you are at this stage, you understood the benefits of estate planning at one time, but perhaps haven't realized how fast the rules can change. Taking time to reassess your situation can give you peace of mind that your original plan is still valid.

Then in column four, **you have a well thought out plan, an executed plan that is completely understood by you, your family, and your financial team**. Complete peace of mind comes from knowing you have a good plan and it will be executed correctly at the time you need it most. If you are in this stage, your family and your team are there for you.

There are so many levels to a well thought out estate plan. Many individuals do not even have the most basic legal documents in place such as wills and trusts. Above and beyond this, estates can become increasingly complicated and complex. Even with proper documents in place, we find many individuals and families do not completely understand what they have, and/or they've not re-evaluated those documents since they were initially drafted years ago.

Once you achieve an ideal score, the proper documents are in place. They are monitored at least annually for any changes and adjustments. And you have a complete understanding of what is contained within the documents. Additionally, an attorney qualified to meet your unique needs generally has or should become part of your overall trusted team of advisors.

Mindset Number Eight: Charitable Planning

Mindset 8: Charitable Plan	
You make periodic charitable contributions, but you do not have any established plans while living or at death	1 2 3
You have plans to establish a set schedule for charitable gifts while living and/or at death	4 5 6
You have current established plans for charitable giving while living or at death but this needs to be updated or you have not evaluated all of the options and benefits to make gifts you desire	7 8 9
You have a well-thought-out plan regarding charitable giving. This could include a cognizant decision not to give while living and/or at death	10

Score:	
Ideal:	

In column one of Mindset Eight, **you make periodic charitable contributions, but you do not have any established plans while living or at death**. Giving, at this stage, is either something you've actively declined to pursue (in which case, as earlier, a low score is not a problem) or it is done without forming part of a larger plan. At this stage both you and the charity or charities of your choosing could be losing out.

Column two, **you have plans to establish a set schedule for charitable gifts while living and/or at death**. Contributing on a schedule is a great way to begin and to reinforce the habit to give regularly. At this stage, you have not assessed whether the way you are giving is most beneficial.

Column three, **you have currently established plans for charitable giving while living or at death, but this needs to be updated, or, you have not evaluated all the options and benefits to making charitable gifts if you desire to do so.** At this stage, you have a well-defined plan, however it may have been some time since it was reviewed. In addition, your charitable donations may not be in line with your broader goals. Perhaps, a more efficient strategy may be an option.

Column four, **you have a well-thought-out plan regarding charitable giving.** This could include a conscious decision not to give while living and/or at death. You are confident you have made the right decisions and your charitable giving is regularly reviewed and performed in the most beneficial and efficient way.

This is another mindset which is not of interest to everybody we speak with. If you have no charitable inclination, then there's really no need to have a perfect score on this, which is why if you've decided you're not interested in making charitable contributions, that scores a 10 as well.

For many reasons, there may be significant benefits to making charitable contributions, depending on your estate situation, including potential tax benefits.

Many people have a charitable inclination but have not gone through the process of evaluating the best options to make this a seamless process.

The goal should be to establish what your charitable desires are both while your living and at death, and to determine the best way to make this happen from a tax, legal, and personal preference standpoint.

There are many different ways to structure charitable gifts, depending on a number of factors including the value of your estate, how charitable giving might reduce tax burdens, and whether you wish to receive an income from your gift while you're living.

Figuring out what's important and achieving the best outcomes for your situation are part of the process of doing a deep dive into your charitable planning needs.

Mindset Number Nine: Family Continuity

Mindset 9: Family Continuity	
Nobody has an understanding of our family wealth	1
	2
	3
There is only one person with a thorough understanding of our family wealth and planning strategies	4
	5
	6
Both spouses have a thorough understanding of your wealth but the family has not been included in these discussions	7
	8
	9
Both spouses and family members have a complete understanding of your wealth and overall planning strategies now and at death	10

Score:	
Ideal:	

The continuity of your family wealth is the focus of Mindset Nine. In the first column, **nobody has an understanding of your family wealth**. The least considered approach may be causing you the most stress. We often see wealth being a difficult subject for families to discuss, so if you score low in this mindset, don't despair. Even if you have never had a conversation before, you can use this scorecard to start a discussion.

Column two, **there is only one person with a thorough understanding of your family wealth and planning strategies**. Ensuring someone else in the family has an understanding of the situation is vitally important should anything happen to you. Often, for people at this stage, this is a spouse or accountant. While this is a good start, improving your score by ensuring those with an understanding are in a position to act on this information is a great start.

Column three, **both spouses have a thorough understanding of your wealth, but the family has not been included in these discussions**. True legacy wealth is achieved when all the family are aware of, and on board with your plans. In this stage, it is a great starting point that both spouses have a clear understanding of the family's continuity plans. However, if one of you passes, or, even worse, if something happens to both of you, ensuring the family are all on board beforehand, can give you peace of mind that your plans for the continuity of your family wealth will be executed in accordance with your wishes.

Column four, **both spouses and family members have a complete understanding of your wealth, and overall plan and strategies now and at death**. A comprehensive team approach to wealth requires not only trusted advisors, but a strong family team. In this stage, you have confidence the family wealth will survive no matter what happens.

There are typically two components we address with this particular question. The first is, "Are both spouses completely aware of how the overall wealth management plan is structured?"

We often see that one spouse is completely in control of all the planning, including investments, legal documents, tax planning, etc. While it's not always necessary for the other spouse to be as involved, we feel it's extremely important for what I call the 'uninvolved spouse' to understand and be comforted by the fact that all of that planning has been taken care of.

Again, working with a trusted advisor, your family's CFO or quarterback if you will, to help ensure all these components are in place, can add to your peace of mind in retirement.

The second component we address is engaging other family members. We're typically talking about children, and our experience has shown that most children are not very well informed about the overall financial situation of their parents.

Our process looks to assist in making the children or other beneficiaries as aware as our clients' desire. Having this process in place is an easy way to transition what's going to happen to your estate not only when either the husband or wife passes, but also when the second spouse dies.

Mindset Number Ten:
Simplicity and Peace of Mind

Mindset 10: Simplicity and Peace Of Mind	
Your financial planning overwhelms you. You spend too much time worrying about it and do not have the peace of mind you desire	1
	2
	3
You do not pay much attention to your financial situation leading to a lack of confidence and peace of mind	4
	5
	6
You have confidence in your overall situation but could benefit from a consolidated strategy to provide you with clarity and peace of mind	7
	8
	9
You have confidence in your overall financial situation which provides you with the peace of mind to live life fully	10

Score:	
Ideal:	

Finally, mindset number 10 is something I've been talking about and reiterating throughout this book: achieving simplicity and peace of mind in your retirement. Column one says **your financial planning overwhelms you. You spend too much time worrying about it and do not have the peace of mind you desire**. People in this stage usually know they need to do something but don't have any idea what or where to find help.

Column two, **you do not pay much attention to your financial situation, leading to a lack of confidence and peace of mind**. In this stage you perhaps have some support, but you lack any motivation to address the situation. This may be because of problems or complexity, but usually comes down to not having the right team in place.

Column three, **you have confidence in your overall situation but could benefit from a consolidated strategy to provide you with clarity and peace of mind.** This is a transitional stage. We often find people here either work with their existing team to raise the bar on the support they are getting, or make the decision they need a new team who can provide the support they need. If you are here, you can often feel the peace of mind that is just within reach.

Column four, **you have confidence in your overall financial situation which provides you with the peace of mind to live life fully**.

This is the most confident, relaxed position to be in. Even if you have scored lower than you would like in earlier mindsets, a high score here means you have the confidence in your team, and now you have a roadmap to address outstanding areas of concern.

This mindset sounds simple, but the truth is simplicity and peace of mind are not very common among people with whom we've had initial discussions. If you were to poll different clients of ours, and ask what value they've gotten from their retirement scorecard in the short time they've been using it, I'm confident 'peace of mind' would be near, if not at, the top of the list.

I talk a lot about adding value in the way I serve my clients and help them prepare for retirement. I cannot imagine creating more value than that which comes from having a simple, well-understood plan that encompasses all the facets of their financial well-being, to ensure they are in the best position possible to enjoy the retirement they deserve.

The WealthCare™ Retirement Scorecard Effect

Does this really work? I'd like to share an example with you.

I had a meeting with a longtime client recently. He's a business owner, transitioning to retirement. His son will be taking over the running of the business. His wife is not actively involved either in the business or in their overall financial landscape.

This is a client I've worked closely with for years, and in that time we've not only touched individually on all of the 10 mindsets which are included in the scorecard, we've dug pretty deeply into them.

Even with that history, completing the retirement scorecard highlighted one area which was weak. It was mindset number 10, which is simplicity and peace of mind. As we walked through his scorecard, I knew his legal documents were where they needed to be, the business planning was where it needed to be, the family continuity was where it needed to be. He has a great tax advisor. Financially, he and his wife have enough money to retire and live however they want to. I knew all of that was in place, but as we progressed it became increasingly clear that my client didn't.

As we walked through the mindsets on the scorecard, and he responded with a lower score in some situations than I had expected, I was surprised.

If he gave himself a lower score regarding his legal documents, I didn't interrupt and say we actually have done those. I just let him talk. Similarly, as we looked at his ideal scores, and yet, I knew, his scores across the board were a little bit higher, I didn't interrupt.

Once he finished his assessment of where he was, and where he wanted ideally to be, we had the opportunity to look over each of the mindsets and discuss the challenges he was (or thought he was) having.

When we walked away from that meeting, he actually shook my hand, gave me a hug, and said "You know what, I can't tell you how much better I feel right now, but more importantly how much more confidence I have that we've done everything or most everything we need to do. We're on the right track. I can't wait to go home and tell my wife that we've had this meeting. Although she's not involved with this very much, she does worry about it. Every time she asks me a question, I haven't had that confidence to say yes we've got all this taken care of."

As an advisor, it's a truly rewarding to see a client go through the scorecard process and begin making needed transitions in areas that will give him or her greater peace of mind. But this particular client brought home to me that just because I have confidence that my client is in great shape, my client may not have that same confidence.

Without the scorecard, and taking time to run through these mindsets together, he may not have shared my understanding that things were well taken care of and all necessary actions were being taken to help ensure his family's financial future. For him, it was transformative.

One note. It isn't only the amount of money you have that gives you peace of mind about your financial health. I know people who are never, ever going to have to worry about money for the rest of their lives. Yet, some of them worry more than people who have a tenth or a hundredth of their 'wealth'.

In fact, many of those we work with are not ultra-high net worth clients. The peace of mind they receive from knowing they have the ability to maintain their lifestyle well into retirement is amazing.

Once you complete the Ruggie WealthCare™ scorecard, you should find your personal pain points. Maybe you need to re-examine your legal documents, or learn more about your long-term care insurance. Perhaps you need to make sure your family is clear about your financial situation and planning strategies in the event something happens to you.

The scorecard puts you in the position to recognize your shortfalls and prioritize which you'd like to address first. It presents them in a consolidated view which allows you to address concerns and track your progress over time.

The most important step is understanding your mindsets. From there you can take actions that will have a tremendous impact on the health of your wealth, and on your overall peace of mind, throughout your retirement years.

Your WealthCare™ Retirement Scorecard

Here's how to get the most from your scorecard.

For each Mindset, there are four stages, and each stage is divided into a low, middle and high scores.

Your first step is to find which stage resonates with you most.

Then, determine within that stage whether you would give yourself a score on the low end, in the middle or high end.

A lower score would indicate some weakness within that stage and an opportunity to develop it further.

A middle score means you are solidly entrenched in that stage.

A higher score indicates you may be on the verge of transitioning to the next stage.

Where you fall in each Mindset will likely not remain constant throughout the entire scorecard. Also, some Mindsets may seem to reflect only minor differences within a stage, while others may have significant differences – for example between an 8 and a 10.

If you are at a 10 you are completely focused and "in the zone" within that Mindset, whereas if you are at an 8, there may still be plenty of room for improvement.

Here's What to Do Next

When planning for retirement, focusing on one or two indicators to assess how good your financial health is, makes no more sense than focusing only on your blood pressure and heart rate to assess how good your actual health is.

The Ruggie WealthCare™ comprehensive scorecard is the starting point to understanding and improving your financial health in retirement.

This short financial check-up effectively predicts 10 key components of financial health.

1. You have implemented a sound investment strategy with a trusted advisor.
2. Your independent advisor provides access to all types of investments.
3. You're confident you will not outlive your money.
4. You have systematically established continual access to your updated net worth.
5. All insurance options have been properly vetted.
6. Your qualified tax advisor coordinates with your entire financial team.
7. Your well-thought-out estate plan is up-to-date, executed and completely understood.

8. Your charitable/philanthropic plan has been executed and implemented.
9. Both spouses and appropriate family members have a complete understanding of your situation.
10. Your life will be simplified and you will enjoy greater peace of mind.

To get a free assessment of your Ruggie WealthCare™ Retirement Scorecard, go to **www.RuggieWealth.com.**

There, you'll find a version of the scorecard you can complete online. Once you have submitted it, you will be eligible for a free consultation with a Ruggie WealthCare™ Advisor in one of our offices who will help you to better understand where you are in the process of preparing for retirement, the steps you can take on your path to greater financial health, and how to score the best possible financial situation for your retirement years.